The Muted Muse

A Poetry Collection

By
Jocelyne Smallian-Khan

Copyright © 2022
Jocelyne Smallian-Khan / Smallian-Khan Ltd.

All rights reserved. No part of this publication may be reproduced or transmitted in any form or by any means, electronic or mechanical, including photocopying, recording, or any information storage and retrieval system, without express permission in writing from the author/publisher.

For information contact:
   jjsmalliankhan@gmail.com
   http://www.jjsk.ca

ISBN: 978-1-7780584-0-0
First Print Edition: January 2022

Blocked

The ribbon, runs dry
  The muse, is mute

Jocelyne Smallian-Khan

The Muted Muse

Table of Contents

Inarticulate 2
Dreamtype 3
Silent Typewriter 4
The Muse 5
At the desk 6
Quiet Lizard 7
Blank Canvas 8
Blank Paper 9
Remembering 10
Retreat 11
Delete, delete... 12
Driverless 13
So Much Rage 14
Human Failure 15
I think… 16
Creative Drought 17
Diversion 18
Silence 19
2AM 20
Noaughts 21
Adam 22
Pretense 23
About the Author 24
More from Jocelyne 25

Inarticulate

The itch of an idea
Prickling in my brain
It scurries and scrabbles into corners
Eluding catch…
Eluding scratch…

The sting of inspiration swells
Throbbing, throbbing
My pulse beats with a need to create
Something…
Anything…

A slice of insight
Slashing my soul
My gasping psyche stretches out
Reaching…
Screeching…
Beseeching…

Dreamtype

I have been dreaming of typewriters
Old manual Underwoods
And electric Olivettis
Are appearing nocturnally
In my mind's meanderings

Remington reminiscences

Chunka-chuka and clickity-clickty
   Pages rolling up and down
          ziiip... ziiip
    Striiitch... Thunkkk... Dinggg

Maybe my mind is telling me
That I should step away
From the computer
And get reacquainted
With an old friend

      ...Dinggggg

Silent Typewriter

Clicking keys once chanted
The tapping's taciturn
The ribbon has run dry
My muse is rendered mute

The Muse

Writer's block is my muse
Lighting my creative fuse
The thing I write about most
Is having nothing to write about

At the desk

Sitting at the desk
Struggling with pen in hand
Get over yourself

Quiet Lizard

Just three lines
Not so tough
Shut up Lizard

Blank Canvas

I paint in blue ink
The white page is my canvas
The canvas is blank

Blank Paper

Blue ink ballpoint pen
Giving no revelations
On blank white paper

Remembering

Time to reminisce
The recall of what once was
Is memory real?

Retreat

Mark
     and erase
Speak
     and retract
Retroactive
     hesitation

Delete, delete

False starts and retracing steps
The backspace key is my enemy
I erase it because I hate it
And once it is gone I am sorry

Driverless

The motivation fizzles
The inspiration's dead
The muse no longer sizzles
The drive has turned to dread

So Much Rage

Raging road rages
Raging digital rages
Raging rages into echoes
Raging rages against time
Raging rages on blank pages
Raging rages against The Man
Raging rages Bringing The Noise
Raging rages Against The Machine
Raging rages against the Dying of the Light

Rages Raging For What? Most of All -
Rages Raging Against Myself.

Human Failure

To accept failing
Unable to fulfill
The most basic
Human function
Obliged, compelled
How to compensate
For such inadequacy

I think…

So now where should I start
Pick it apart
Brain fart
Descartes
Breaking my heart
No guarantees in art

Creative Drought

Turned out
Burned out
Check out
Chill out

All out
Back out
Self doubt
No clout

Diversion

A diversion
A distraction
A digital reaction

It came and went
Not time well spent

Thanks for the memories
Anyway

Silence

The whistle whine
        gets louder over time
Auditory overload
        pulsing morse code
Ignored abjectly
        transmitted directly
Again and again
        into the brain
Mind made dull
        by echo in skull
Devoured drowned
        engulfed in sound
Appreciate in defiance
        what may soon become silence

2AM

It's 2AM
and here I am
Awake again

It wouldn't be so bad
Except I will still be here
3 hours from now
Awake still
And having to get up
for work in the morning

Sleep comes easy
At 2PM
Afternoon retreat
Snuggle in sweet sleep
Out like a light for 3 hours straight

But at 2AM, here I am
Awake again

Maybe I'm living in the wrong time zone
And am meant to be on the other side of the globe
Where it's *2PM* now
And I can be awake during daytime
And sleep at nighttime
Like decent people are supposed to do

But instead of being there
I am here
Here I am
at 2AM
Awake again

Noaughts

```
Naughts
o
t
s
          Nots
          a
          u
          g
          h
          t
          s
                    N
                    o
               Naughts
                    s
     N
     a
     u
     g
     h
     Nots
     s         N
               o
               t
            Naughts
        N
        a
        u
        g
        h
        t
     Nots
```

Adam

How curious it must be
To be your father's son
Flesh of a legend

Is there expectation
That you will somehow
Be the second coming

Are you called
To create
To recreate

Does his shadow
Loom over
Your path

Or are you free
To be
Who you want to be

About the Author

The pandemic lockdown and an online poetry workshop helped Jocelyne Smallian-Khan re-ignite an old pastime of playing around with words purely for creative enjoyment. After 30 years of spending her writing time on decidedly less artistic pieces such as essays, business cases, briefing notes, strategic plans, Treasury Board submissions, Memoranda to Cabinet, and other works of mundanity, she has rediscovered a joy in writing poetry. *The Muted Muse* is her first standalone collection of published poems.

She would like to thank David Allan Hamilton, for his Ottawa Writing Workshops (www.ottawawritingworkshops.com), which helped her battle "The Lizard" and begin scribbling poems again after such a long pause.

She would also like to thank Warren Dean Fulton / Gnurr Productions Inc. for being the first to accept some of her poetry for publication in a periodical.

Pretense

I put the booklet
Containing my poems
On my bookshelf

Not with the books about writing
But with the poetry anthologies
Of my university days

How dare I
Sit amongst the likes of
Wordsworth and Pope
Coleridge and Poe

The brazenness
Of sharing a shelf with
Shakespeare and Cummings
Atwood and Cohen

It was an act
           Of rebellion
               Of defiance
                    Of self-affirmation

More from Jocelyne

More of Jocelyne's poems can be found in:

It Sounded Like Darkness: a poetry collection (David Allan Hamilton, editor, DeeBee Books, April 2021); available on Amazon

Pocket Lint: a little lit magazine, Issue # 1 (Warren Dean Fulton/Gnurr Productions Inc, April 2021 available from pocketlint2021@gmail.com

Pocket Lint: a little lit magazine, Issue # 2 (Warren Dean Fulton/Gnurr Productions Inc, July 2021) available from pocketlint2021@gmail.com

Rain Dropped Softly: A Poetry Collection, (David Allan Hamilton, editor, December 2021) available on Amazon

Forthcoming

Dancing Words: A Poetry Collection (Jocelyne Smallian-Khan, fall 2022)

www.ingramcontent.com/pod-product-compliance
Lightning Source LLC
Chambersburg PA
CBHW050506120526
44589CB00046B/2007